Inside the Tortoise Shell

Written by H. Carter Mondy
Illustrated by K. Michael Crawford

ISBN 0-9723464-06

Printed in Korea

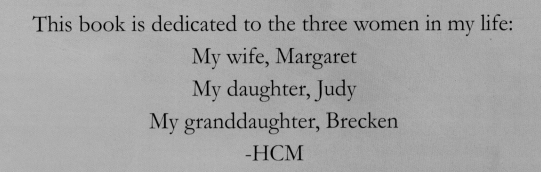

This book is dedicated to the three women in my life:
My wife, Margaret
My daughter, Judy
My granddaughter, Brecken
-HCM

For all those who believed in me
and helped me along the way.

•

A special thanks to Carol McKenzie,
for all your magical help!
-KMC

I wonder what it's like inside
The tortoise shell where the tortoise hides--

Does he have pictures in the hall,
Or carpeting from wall to wall?

And where does the tortoise
sleep at night,
And does he have an electric light?

Does he have an oven in
which to bake
His cookies, or a pie,
or maybe a cake?

On rainy days do you suppose
He uses a nail file on his toes?

I've looked long and could not see
An antenna for his TV.

I often wonder it he hath
A tub in which to take a bath,

Or if the doorbell
ever rings
When in the shower
the tortoise sings?

Do you suppose he has a phone
To call his friends when they're at home?

I guess these things I'll not be knowin',
for he never comes out so I can go in.

So Long!